COACHING 9, 10 AND 11 YEAR OLDS

By

Bobby Howe

and

Tony Waiters

World of Soccer
Vancouver

First published 1989 by WORLD OF SOCCER

Phone: (604) 921-8963 Fax: (604) 921-8964
Information Service: 1-800-762-2378

First printing August, 1989
Second printing June, 1990
Third printing September, 1991
Fourth printing February, 1993
Fifth printing September, 1994
Sixth printing October, 1995
Seventh printing April, 1997

CREDITS
Editor: Bob Dunn
Illustrator: Martin Nichols
Copy Processing: Barbara Schiffner
Layout and Design: Dunn Communications Ltd.

Manufactured by Hemlock Printers Ltd.

Canadian Cataloguing in Publication Data
Howe, Bobby.
Coaching 9, 10 and 11 year olds
(Coaching series)
Includes bibliographical references and index.
ISBN 1-896466-02-8
1. Soccer for children – Coaching. I. Waiters, Tony
II. Title.   III. Title: Coaching nine, ten and eleven year olds. IV. Series.
GV943.8.H67 1993   796.334'07'7   C95-900993-0

THE COACHING SERIES:

Coaching 6, 7 and 8 year olds

Coaching 9, 10 and 11 year olds

Coaching the Team

Coaching the Goalkeeper

Coaching the Player

OTHER WORLD OF SOCCER PUBLICATIONS:

Teaching Offside

Soccer is Fun #1, #2 & #3 – Workbooks for 6, 7 and 8 Year Olds

Micro Soccer – Rules & Regulations

Hotshots #1, #2 & #3 – Workbooks for 9, 10 and 11 Year Olds

Ace Coaching Cards

Zonal Defending – The Flat Back Four

ACKNOWLEDGEMENTS

Sharleen King
Joanie Komura
Jerry Capodanno
Gerald Guthrie
Rob Walker
The Silver Bullets Soccer Team

DEDICATION

This book is dedicated to the young soccer players of the United States and Canada: may they gain as much enjoyment from soccer in the New World as the authors have with their roots in the Old but with their hearts in the "New."

TABLE OF CONTENTS

1. **INTRODUCTION**
    The Ages of Soccer 6
    The Golden Age of Learning 8
    The Practice Session 9
    The Soccer Sandwich 10
    Be Prepared 11
    What to Teach 12
    The Coach 13
    The Game is the Teacher 16
    Third Man Running 20

2. **THE HOWE WAY**
    Game One 24
    Game Two 25
    Game Three 26
    Game Four 27
    Game Five 28
    Game Six 29
    Game Seven 30
    Game Eight 31
    Game Nine 32
    Game Ten 33

3. **MASTERING TECHNIQUES**
    The Shape of Things to Come 34
    What are the Key Techniques 35
    Passing 35
    Control 37
    Heading 38
    Shooting 38
    Tackling 39
    Dribbling 39

4. **THE WAITERSWAY**
    Micro Soccer 41
    The Zone Game 42
    The Four-Goal Game 43
    Chip 'n Dale 44
    Criss-Cross 45
    Side Kicks 46
    Through Balls 47
    The Three-Shot Stop 48
    Noah's Lark 49
    Square Pegs 50

5. **THE AGE OF SKILL**
    Individual Possession 51
    Combining to Keep Possession 53

6. **SIMPLE DEFENDING**
    1 vs 1 56
    2 vs 2 58

7. **APPENDIX**
    The Game is the Teacher 59
    Coaching Through the Kids' Eyes 59
    Organization of the Practice 60
    Why 3-a-side? Why 4-a-side? 61
    Social Groups 61
    Offside 62
    Equipment 62
    Not The Golden Age of Heading 63
    Bibliography 63
    Planning a Season's Program 64

INTRODUCTION

The Ages of Soccer

Children who play soccer from an early age will usually pass through four distinct phases before they become mature (adult) soccer players.

The Beginner

In the Western World, children generally enter into some form of organized soccer — either at school or within the community — at around age 6 (Grade 1). These early years (6 to 8) should be considered the Beginner Phase. During this time, children learn to kick the ball in a comfortable, co-ordinated way, to run purposefully with the ball, and to begin playing as a team against other children. They are just starting to understand the need to share the ball (passing), to help one another to go forward (offense), and to combine to stop the opposition (defense).

However, it must be understood that players at this age are just emerging from a colossal growth and development period … i.e. from being born to going to school … a relatively short space of time in which they have learned to crawl, walk, run and talk. In soccer terms, when they start the game for the first time, they are still "babies" — relatively uncoordinated, understandably egocentric, and so view their world of soccer from that perspective.

This important age period was covered in the first book of the "Coaching" series. Great emphasis was placed on the games and practices recommended, in making sure the kids had fun, and felt good about themselves and the game of soccer.

The Pre-Teen Phase (9, 10 and 11)

The second soccer stage sees the young soccer player emerging from the beginner phase around 8 or 9 years of age. Coaches of these players finds themselves faced by eager, coordinated, energetic youngsters who are like sponges in their ability and willingness to learn, but who want to learn by "doing" not by being lectured; whose relationship with their parents, teachers and coaches is at an optimum. It is, without doubt "The Golden Age of Learning" and this stage in the lives of the young soccer players is the most important in terms of skills development.

Golden Age Kids are all Players and Goalkeepers

Players should not be wingers, strikers or fullbacks at this time in their soccer development and experience. Nor should there be a permanently-positioned and recognized team goalkeeper. These youngsters are **soccer players**. They are not even attackers, midfielders or defenders.

The duty of the coach is to give each player the opportunity to develop all the skills of the game — including goalkeeping. Positions and positional play will begin in earnest with the move into 11-a-side soccer — hopefully at 12 years of age.

The Early Teens (12 – 15)

Through necessity we have generalized in terms of the age classifications. We all know that children do not mature at the same rate. However, for most, the early adolescence years are between 12 – 15. In many ways, this time in the life of young people can be described as the "turbulent years."

It is usually a period of great change both physically and psychologically, with an accompanying increasing resistence to authority — parent, coach and teacher. Normally there is a rapid skeletal growth (with accompanying increased danger of injuries); youngsters relate to one another (peer pressure) better than with adults; they are becoming accustomed to working and socializing in larger groups (gangs). Coaching this age group requires a very different approach to the 1st two phases with the "team" aspect becoming much more important: the coach must be skillful so as not to alienate his/her somewhat already erratic and unpredictable young charges. The trauma and the distractions of the "early teens" only further emphasize how important "The Golden Age of Learning" is in building a base of all-round soccer skills.

The Later Teens (16 – 19)

As teenagers grow through the early adolescent stages, in most cases the growth spurt upwards slows down and the rest of the body has the chance to catch up with the skeletal growth. We can expect a change of attitude as the more mature teenager sees adulthood and a career not too far away. This is another good phase in the soccer development process — particularly for the serious and committed soccer player. Much can be accomplished by the coach with regard to Team Development and the Tactical Role of the Individual within the team.

Boys and Girls — Together?

In the manual "Coaching 6, 7 and 8 Year Olds", Tony Waiters and Bobby Howe maintained there was no reason why boys and girls should not play together at that age. In fact, they recommended it. Some clubs have a policy that boys and girls play separately; there are other clubs for "Boys Only" or "Girls Only."

It is the feeling of Waiters and Howe that as players enter the "Golden Age of Learning", boys and girls should begin to separate in soccer — if they have not already. It may not be really necessary for the 9 year olds or the 10 year olds, but as young soccer players approach the "Early Teen" phase, certain contra-characteristics of play begin to show between the two sexes. The boys tend to take a more physical ("macho") approach to the game while, with the girls, the physical side is nowhere near as important.

THE GOLDEN AGE OF LEARNING

In "The Golden Age of Learning," Bobby Howe and Tony Waiters have studied the priorities for coaching 9, 10 and 11 year olds. They have emphasized the importance of technique practice and have provided examples of realistic and challenging games that will assist players in their understanding of the game and help to improve their levels of skill.

The subtitle of this manual is consistent with the beliefs of most educators, that the age group 9 – 11 observes the important crossover from "selfishness" to the ability to socialize. In soccer terms, through this age period, children learn to understand the importance of cooperation in team play.

This coaching manual is the sequel to the first book written by the authors, entitled "Coaching 6, 7 and 8 Year Olds." Howe and Waiters are aware that in many cases the coaches at the "Golden Age" phase are the same ones who started with the team when the children first began soccer two or three years ago, coaches who are hoping to advance the players' progress — and their own development as coaches.

However, Howe and Waiters realize this will not always be the case as a significant percentage of coaches in the 9, 10 and 11 year old player bracket will be "first time coaches." Whether you are a "first time" or a "veteran coach," you may not have seen their first book. In that respect one major objective of this manual is to present the information in such a way that the information can stand on its own and communicate to readers whatever their backgrounds and knowledge.

If you already have the first manual, the practices recommended will work just as well for this older group. You will also be able to see the "progressions" made from the practices in the first book to the 20 recommended games in this manual.

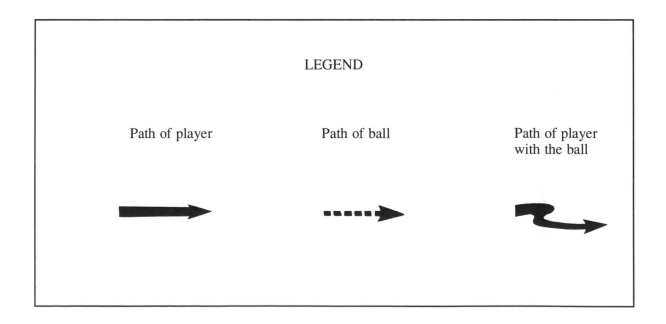

LEGEND

| Path of player | Path of ball | Path of player with the ball |

THE PRACTICE SESSION

Essential Ingredients: Practice Must Be Stimulating, Challenging — and Fun!

In our first manual (Coaching 6, 7 and 8 Year Olds), there was a description of the ingredients required in practice to provide for the kids — a FEAST!

These considerations of the FEAST do not change just because the players grow older — whether it's a practice session for 9, 10 and 11 year olds or professionals preparing for the World Cup.

There will however, be a change of emphasis as they mature as soccer players.

In "The Golden Age," there should be a greater emphasis on "skills development" — still laced with generous portions of fun, activity and team play if the session is to be enjoyable and successful.

A FEAST

Fun — has to be an essential requirement of every exercise, at every practice.

Everyone — must receive an equal opportunity of involvement — in other words, equal time.

Activity — must be at the core of the soccer sessions, because it affects every other part of the FEAST.

Skills — must be developed for greater enjoyment of soccer, through greater accomplishment.

Team play — must be included in every activity, because soccer is a "team" game.

Obtaining the right balance in the practice session is very important. Coaches should do everything possible during the practice session to send every player home enthused about soccer — and looking forward to the next practice or game.

6, 7 and 8's	—	Greatest emphasis on Fun
9, 10 and 11's	—	Most important age for Skills Development
12 onwards	—	Development of Team Play and Role of Individual

THE SOCCER SANDWICH

One old coach describing the soccer development process used to say: "There are many ways up Everest." And so there are! But some routes give a greater chance of success than others.

To make the practice session stimulating and fun for the 9, 10 and 11 year old, consider using the following format:

Introductory Activity

7 – 10 min.

This is a lively start to the first minutes of practice. For instance, a ball for each player introducing different dribbling and juggling activities; or pairs activities — dribbling and passing. Plenty of ACTION AND ACTIVITY to get the players off and running and bubbling — a tasty **hors d'oeuvres**.

Game

10 – 15 min.

Children want to play. Set up a "game" activity or practice that gives them the opportunity to do just that. See the Howe Way and the WaitersWay segments for "games" that are fun but develop certain skills just by "playing."

Skills Practice

10 – 12 min.

Having identified your "objectives" for the practice session, take 10 minutes to concentrate on one or two skills developers (see pages 24–33 and 41–50 for practice ideas).

Game

12 – 15 min.

The end-of-session scrimmage is often seen as a "free-er," less structured opportunity for fun and self-expression where the coaches can join in, too. While larger numbers (eg. 7 vs 7) reduce the number of potential ball touches per player and therefore skills development opportunities, the competitive, challenging and fun finale more than compensates for that.

The Soccer Sandwich, well presented and with the right ingredients, will be well-accepted. But don't give children "soccer indigestion" by oversized portions of the game or of skills practice.

Remember the "bread and butter" of soccer is the "game." The "meat" of the practice is the "skills" segment in the middle.

With changeovers from practice to practice, a session with the format suggested will take as little as 45 minutes and no longer than 60. Just about right for 9, 10 and 11 year olds!

BE PREPARED

GET READY!

- Try to find 10 or 15 minutes in your busy schedule to plan the session.
- List the objectives of session: the games and practices to be enjoyed.
- Anticipate numbers of players, field conditions, time for the session and each individual practice, number of soccer balls, and equipment needs.

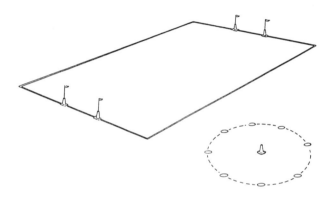

GET SET!

- Arrive early if you can.
- Set out as much of practice areas as possible before you start, so that the session runs smoothly and the transition from one practice to another is not disruptive.
- If you cannot arrive early, have an assistant or parent set up the area for you — possibly during your introductory activity.
- Do not have players standing around at the start of practice waiting for something to happen.

GO!

- Supervise and encourage.
- "Coach" if you are confident of your information and have a sense of occasion; flexibility and adaptability (i.e. if weather changes) are qualities of a good coach.

WHAT TO TEACH

The objectives of the coach

In our first book, we described the "essential skills" of the game of soccer. However, there is another major requirement beyond "basic skill" if players are to develop — that is the **understanding** required to function together as a "team." The players are now 9, 10 and 11 years old and have a greater possibility for coordinated effort.

ESSENTIAL SKILLS	GOLDEN AGE OF LEARNING	UNDERSTANDING OF "TEAM PLAY"
Kicking — Passing, Shooting, Crossing	The ideal time for relating the basic skills to "GAME" situations.	**Rules** of the game
Ball "Handling" Skills — Ball Control, Dribbling	Moving the "How" to the "When," "Where," "With Whom," "Against Whom."	**Combined Play** — Effective Offense, Effective Defense
1 vs 1 Defending		**Restarts** — Free Kicks, Corners, Throw-ins
Heading	Practices in situations players can understand i.e. 3 vs 1, 2 vs 2, 3 vs 3, 4 vs 2.	
Throw-in technique		
Goalkeeping — Diving, Catching, Kicking, Throwing		**Goalkeeper** Responsibilities within the team.

The Golden Age — bridges the gap

Activity with others — involving cooperation and communication — will always be less than perfect. So the bridge from simple technique work — such as from **how** to kick, **how** to control to the **WITH WHOM, WHEN, WHERE, WHY** — is one of the major objectives in the "Golden Age." In coaching "understanding," it should not be too complicated — by large numbers of players, even some of the rules (e.g. offside). At this stage, an important part of the coaching methodology is to develop the skills of soccer in game-related situations.

THE COACH

Introduction

In "Coaching 6, 7 and 8 Year Olds," we made the point that THE GAME IS THE GREAT TEACHER.

If that's the case, then what is the role of the coach?

Perhaps the coach should be considered an assistant to the game in teaching the players and an assistant to the players in their understanding of the game.

How does the coach interpret the game? How does the coach help the players solve their problems?

Organization

The coach should spend a little time before each session preparing the practice. This can't be emphasized too much. Good practice preparation should consider the following points:

- The theme
- Number of players
- Equipment needs (balls, bibs, goals, cones, wosmarkers, etc.)
- Available field space
- Practice progression
- Time allotted for each practice segment.

If the coach is not prepared before practice, coaching time during the practice will be displaced by organizational time. When disorganized, a coach's credibility may hang in the balance.

Demonstration

"A picture paints a thousand words."

In a practice, the coach must:

- Understand one's own abilities before attempting to demonstrate;

- Demonstrate exactly what is expected from the players, use capable players to demonstrate, or "walk through" the demonstration so that it's a true "picture" of the technique.

A good demonstration is crucial to ensuring that players understand what they are supposed to accomplish in the practice. Good demonstrations increase the credibility of the coach in the eyes of the players and also motivate the players to perform the techniques properly.

Observation and information

The skill of coaching is to observe the mistakes of players as individuals, or as a team, and to provide the information to correct the mistakes.

There may be times that, individually or as a team, players make mistakes that the coach has observed but is unsure how to correct. In those cases, it is much better for the coach to say nothing and allow the practice to continue, rather than confuse the players AND the coach.

When coaching, remember these key points:

- Supervise

- The game is the best teacher

- Use this book as a resource

- If uncertain of causes of mistakes let practice proceed.

Coaching information should be clear and precise. A long, drawn-out explanation of a mistake will cause players to lose attention.

Naturally, many mistakes occur in practice games. However, it would be poor judgment for the coach to stop the game every time a mistake is made. The players must be allowed to play. Too many "interruptions" will cause players to lose attention. ONE OF THE ARTS OF GOOD COACHING IS KNOWING WHEN TO STOP PLAY AND WHEN TO ALLOW PLAY TO CONTINUE.

Method

- Coaching 9, 10 and 11 year olds requires attention in all aspects of the game. However, one practice session cannot cover all areas.

- Practices should be realistic and developed to highlight one theme. For example, if BALL CONTROL is the theme of the practice, the players should be controlling balls much of the time.

- Coaching requires that players are motivated and challenged. Observing their mistakes and weaknesses and encouraging their successes stimulates this process.

- In guiding players towards successful play, coaches should:

    a) Stop play after a major mistake (if confident of the analysis)

    b) Quickly point out the mistake to the player

    c) Demonstrate the correct "picture" to the player(s)

    d) Restart play and allow the player to correct the mistake under similar circumstances.

- If the error is corrected, the coach should allow the play to continue. If the player continues to make a mistake, the coach should remain with the player to give the player the opportunity to succeed. However, the coach should ensure that the CHALLENGE presented to the player is not too difficult. Players will not be motivated to learn if their tasks are too difficult.

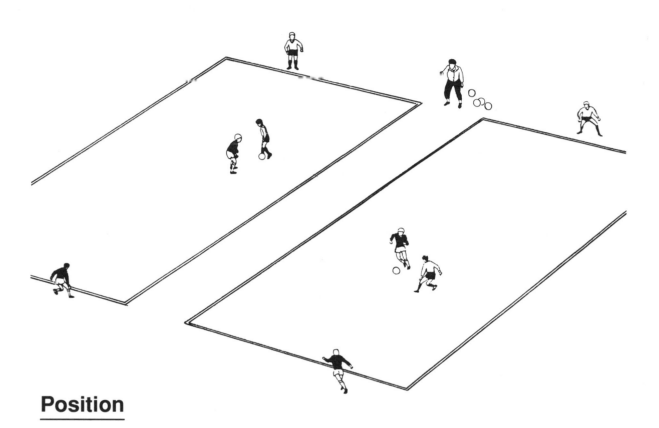

Position

The coach should monitor the practice from "outside" the activity and not in the middle of the play. In a practice session where there is more than one group working, a coach should be positioned to see all the players. When speaking to the players a coach should ensure that the players are facing away from the sun and away from all other activity on the field. Any distraction will cause players to lose attention.

Personality

It is most important that a coach's own personality is reflected in practice sessions and at games. A coach should not try to copy anyone else.

THE GAME IS THE TEACHER

In the manual "Coaching 6, 7 and 8 Year Olds" the importance of placing players in realistic yet enjoyable situations was stressed. The game itself produced learning opportunities and skills development — just by being played!

Micro Soccer — a form of 3-a-side play — was identified as the right place to begin. Over the years the kids of the world have played "street soccer" by improvising the playing conditions. In North America, the circumstances have been very different, and it has been necessary to structure and organize the game. Soccer is not the major sport on this continent as it is in the rest of the world. Consequently, it does not have the profile nor, more importantly, the role models. So the coach should organize *Micro Soccer* for the children, and then let them play! THE GAME IS THE TEACHER.

"Street Soccer" is still a way of life in many regions of the world today — South America, Central America and Africa, for instance. However, in some of the more sophisticated economic areas, the dominance of the automobile, the magnetism of television and the diverse recreational opportunities presented to children have meant that a significant percentage of the young players of the world — even in traditional soccer areas — no longer play "naturally."

In Western Europe, in countries such as Holland, West Germany and the United Kingdom, kids rarely play these days without supervision.

English soccer authorities have felt compelled to set up "Centres of Excellence" to develop young players. Holland has introduced 4-a-side soccer as one of the base development methods. Nonetheless, these countries still retain the advantage of having soccer as the nation's Number One sport — with plenty of role models even if through the medium of television!

In order to replicate the situations that have produced highly-skilled players around the world over the years, coaches of beginner players must ORGANIZE *Micro Soccer*; SUPERVISE the play; ENCOURAGE all players as much as possible ... and keep "coaching" to a minimum.

Micro-Soccer - a form of 3-a-side play

In the 3-a-side game of *Micro Soccer*, simple rules are given (see *Micro Soccer* in WaitersWay Section). Included in each 3-man team is a Goalkeeper, who can also act as a Sweeper. Everyone gets to play in goal on a rotating basis.

In reality, the first-year players find themselves in a 2 vs 2 situation with an additional player on each team — the goalkeeper. This is totally acceptable as 2 "field players" can combine easily together and have the knowledge they have a back supporting player (the goalkeeper) as insurance, should they lose possession of the ball.

As players become more accustomed to the game, encouragement can be given for the goalkeepers to become more involved other than just standing on the goal line. At first it may be no more than the goalkeeper moving a little way off the line to close down the shooting angle for the opposition. Later, the goalkeeper should participate more fully in the 3-player team by taking the role of "sweeper-keeper" — coming out of goal to negate an opposition attack, and/or to help initiate an attack for the team.

The development from goalkeeper to "sweeper-keeper" will take time — maybe as long as 3 years. Again, this is not a problem, and the development should not be forced by the coach — a little encouragement for goalkeepers to do a litle bit more, but still allowing the game to be the main teacher.

The 3-a-side play is the base for player and team development — for the first three years. Not only will the game guarantee each child plenty of kicks of the ball and plenty of fun — but it gives each player a clearly defined and easily understood role within the team triangle. The triangle is the basic tactical consideration and configuration for all team play in soccer — even 11-a-side play.

The logical progression from 3-a-side *Micro Soccer* is to the 4-a-side game. But don't think the progression has to be made too soon. Adding one player to a 3-a-side team does not merely add one more option. Three players can produce only one triangle. Four players produce not only the possibility of four different triangles, but also for those triangles to interchange to produce many permutations.

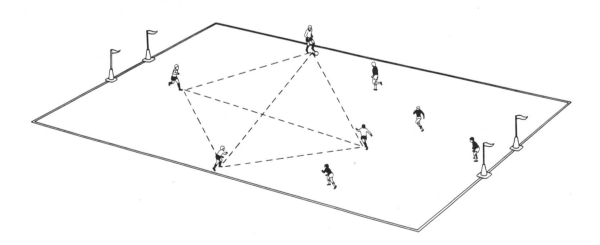

CAUTION SHOULD BE EXERCISED IN PROGRESSING TO 4-A-SIDE AS THE BASE DEVELOPMENT GAME.

1. The roles in 3-a-side *Micro Soccer* are clearly defined (goalkeeper, player with the ball, supporting attacker) and when the ball is passed, it's easy for players to adjust. In 4-a-side, at least one player can be left "off the ball" and confused as to what that player's involvement should be. Even worse, a non-assertive player may stay outside the "team" and play little or no part in the game.

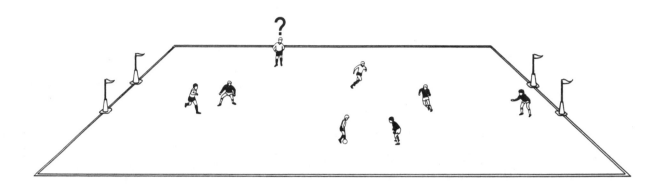

2. To prevent this happening, some coaches intervene by positioning a player in a defending role.

   Negative defending position of "4th" player

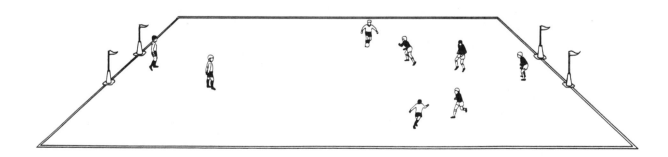

Not only does this deprive the goalkeeper of exciting future possibilities through the extension of the goalkeeping role but it restricts and "condemns" a field player to a negative defensive role. This results in two out-and-out defenders — half the team — (defender + goalkeeper) at too early a time in the players' soccer experience. That can't be right.

3. Professional players given a 4 vs 4 situation would take full advantage of an extra player (compared to 3 vs 3) by having that player in an advanced attacking position, and by doing so, open up many exciting possibilities. As well, it would force the opposition to fall back to mark the advanced attacker and the now more dangerous space created by the attacker in front of the goal. This produces a "diamond" and the attacking value of this shape could not be better termed.

A diamond shape creates valuable attacking possibilities.

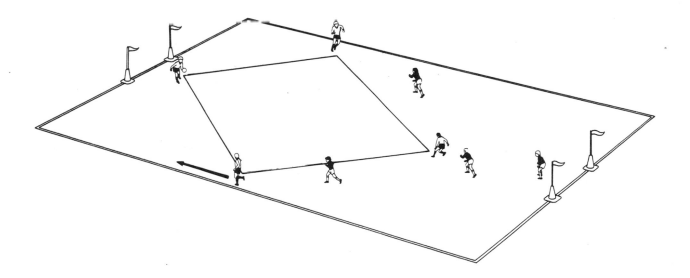

The "extra" player acts as a "target man" for the goalkeeper with the ball, but the goalkeeper still retains the other options of passes (throws/kicks) to the wide-positioned players.

4-a-side requires more from the players in terms of:

- Communication

- Co-operation

- Awareness.

In *Micro Soccer*, the two attacking players (with the goalkeeper back) really need only be aware of one another to produce an effective attacking combination.

In 4-a-side play the three "field players" may find that two is company and three an exciting but more complicated crowd — requiring much more awareness.

It is at this time that the soccer concept known as **Third Man Running** begins to take on importance to young players. Third Man Running is probably the most important attacking concept in the game of soccer. Even professionals have difficulty in mastering and understanding the requirements — and defenders are often tricked by effective exploitation of the Third Man Running.

Third Man Running

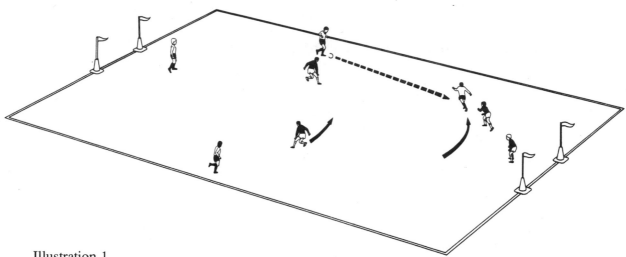

Illustration 1

In illustration 1, the attacking player with the ball is looking to combine with the most advanced player (Target Man). Because of the close proximity of these two players, they should have good eye contact, and it is "natural" for them to play together in this situation. On the opposite side of the field is the Third Man who in the example shown is not in an "open position" to receive the ball — because of the deployment of the opposing defenders.

In illustration 2, the play has developed.

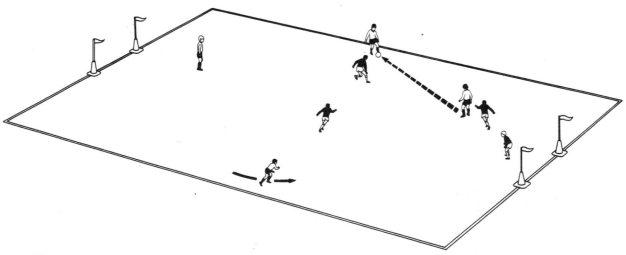

Illustration 2

A "one-two" passing sequence has taken place drawing the opposition towards the action and the ball — a natural inclination for all defenders — giving the opportunity for a diagonal pass to our Third Man who has moved forward on the "blind side" of the defense to provide a scoring chance (see illustration 3, next page).

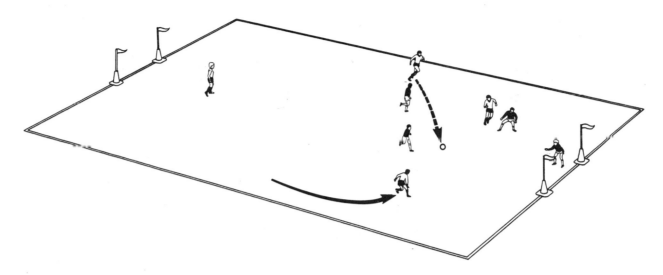

Illustration 3

Of course, defenders will react in different ways. A more experienced defender, for instance, most likely would have been more aware of our Third Man Running, and might have responded as we have shown in illustration 4, thus eliminating the diagonal pass to the attacker.

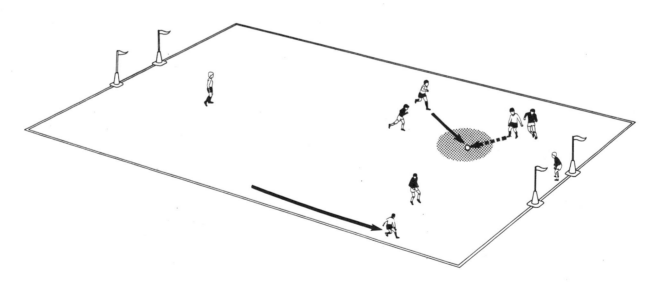

Illustration 4

However, even in this situation, the Third Man Running that takes away a defender has opened up the central attacking space for the player who started the play — to move into position for a return pass from the Target Man and shoot for goal.

As you can see, this is sophisticated stuff. How and why would you explain this to a 6 or 7 year old? Make a run to take both you and a defender away from the action so that your teammate can not only play with the ball but have the ultimate enjoyment of shooting for goal?

These are just two possibilities that could be brought about by "Third Man Running." They have been shown merely to illustrate just how much more complex the game becomes by increasing the base team unit from three to four.

While that addresses the need for increased AWARENESS by all players, two other aspects assume a much greater importance in Team Play through the "Third Man Running" concept:

1. The "timing of the run" — it has to be perfect if the Third Man is to receive the ball unmarked;
2. The "direction and speed" of the pass — they have to be near perfect if the "Third Man's Run" and "the pass" are to coincide to provide the attacking opportunity.

Summary

The time spent here on what happens when the numbers in practice and play are increased from 3 to 4 is important. The 3-a-side games and *Micro Soccer* are used as the basis for developing team play for the 6, 7 and 8 year old.

By extension, the 4-a-side play becomes the base game for 9, 10 and 11 year olds.

The "Third Man Running" concept and 4-a-side play is present in several practices and games in this manual. The idea is to give our "Golden Age" players the opportunity to develop their skills and team play (see pages 33, 42 and 43).

Do not get the impression that players 6 to 11 years of age should play only 3 or 4-a-side. There is great fun to be had towards the end of the practice with the group scrimmaging in 5 vs 5 or 6 vs 6 — with the coaches joining in. In scheduled games in the United States and Canada, Mod Soccer and *Mini Soccer* have team numbers varying from 5 players to 9. This provides great sport.

If players are to develop their skills in team play in a way they can understand, it has to be done in circumstances to which children can relate — otherwise little or no learning will take place. That can be best accomplished in small-sided play.

One more thing should be stressed. If the coach puts the players into fun soccer practices and games such as the ones suggested in this manual, there's no reason to be too concerned about the intricacies of the game. The coach will do a great job by EXPLAINING the rules, the organization and the objectives, SUPERVISING the practice, ENCOURAGING the players. The coach lets them play!

THE GAME IS THE TEACHER.

THE HOWE WAY

In the years that I have worked in the United States, I have been asked by coaches what the differences are between the top class player and the average player.

In general terms, my answer has been that a player must know how to solve the problems that are presented by the game. On offense, a player must understand how to MAINTAIN POSSESSION OF THE BALL and on defense, must have the DESIRE TO WIN THE BALL BACK IMMEDIATELY.

The top player is able to keep possession of the ball under the pressures created by:

1) The moving ball
2) The movement of the body with the ball
3) Opposition
4) Stress.

The average player may struggle when subjected to the above conditions. For example, the average player will "show" the ball to an opponent when trying to take the opponent on or turn the ball towards the opponent when trying to change direction. This may be a result of incorrect practice conditions and playing habits developed at a young age.

The old saying "practice makes perfect" only holds true if players practice correctly. They can practice "correctly" only under the pressures they may expect in a game.

BOBBY HOWE

The technique practices described in this chapter provide simple games that call for repetition of technique but challenge the players to improve performance.

The ages 9, 10 and 11 are the most impressionable. Playing habits can be changed. Therefore, it is important that players learn to play correctly during this period. Bad habits can be changed in young players but are almost impossible to remove as they grow older.

PRACTICE MAKES PERMANENT

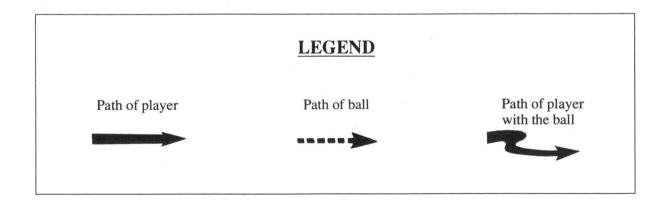

LEGEND

Path of player

Path of ball

Path of player with the ball

Game One

A 3 vs 1 game to develop passing and support

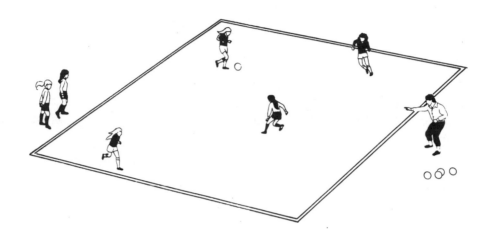

Game Rules

- Three attacking players against one defending player inside an area 10 yards by 10 yards.
- Attacking team tries to keep possession as long as possible.
- Defending team has one player inside the area, and two players outside.
- Attacking team loses possession if the ball goes outside the area or if the defending player makes a tackle or intercepts a pass.
- At loss of possession, defending player is immediately replaced by a teammate.
- Game is over when all defending players have been in the area.
- Number of successful passes accumulated during the three phases is noted.
- Attacking team and defending team change roles.
- Winning team is one with greater number of passes.
- Overall winner is team which first achieves five wins.

NOTE: The coach should have several balls to replace ones kicked out of area.

Player Objectives for Attacking Trio

- Player in possession: to achieve pace, accuracy and timing of pass.
- Supporting players: to time runs to support the player with the ball, and to provide the correct supporting angles.
- All players on offense: to use all available space in the area.

Game Two

A challenging skills practice to develop passing and control

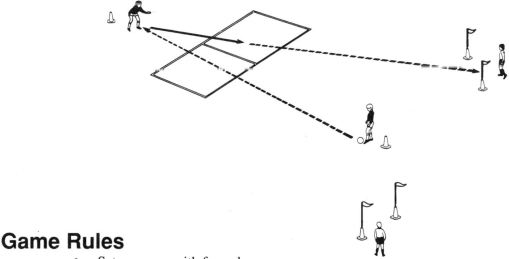

Game Rules

- Set game up with four players.

- Size of grid, size of goals and distance between grid and goals should be determined by coach, according to age/ability of player.
  "The game should be challenging but not impossible!"

- Server plays the ball through grid to receiver.

- Receiver starts five yards behind grid, moves towards ball and plays it with the "first touch" into right side of grid and with the "second touch" (from inside the grid) plays ball through either goal. Next ball is controlled into left side of grid, etc. Players behind goals retrieve balls and return them to server.

- Twenty balls are served.

- Goal counts only if ball is controlled into grid, and played from grid through either goal.

- Player keeps his score.

- Rotate all four players: winner is player to score most goals.

NOTE: If possible have coach or parent as server to give a greater consistency of service.

Player Objectives

- To get a good "first touch" to control and maneuver ball.

- To pass accurately.

NOTE: As players improve, the service may be varied (thrown) so that players have to deal with balls out of the air as well as on the ground.

Game Three

A game to develop heading technique

Game Rules

- Set up game with four players.
- Goal is three yards wide and distance between goal and dotted lines is four yards: dimensions may be varied according to age/ability level of players.
- One team competes against the other, alternating as either "Heading team" or "Goalkeeping team."
- Coach serves ball GENTLY from four yards in the air alternately to players who must HEAD BALL from BEHIND respective lines and try to score.
- Goalkeeper is changed after 10 "head shots."
- After 20 serves (10 to each player), teams change.
- Winning team is one to score more goals.

NOTE: The coach dictates the quality and variation of the service.

Player Objectives

- To be light on feet and adjust to line of ball.
- To look at ball at all times and "throw the eyes" towards it.
- To head ball down towards the goal.

Game Four

A 1 vs 1 game to encourage defending

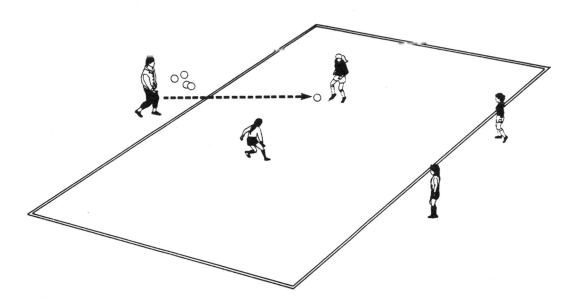

Game Rules

- Set up game in area 10 x 15 yards.
- Organize two teams of two or three players: one player from each team is in area.
- Coach plays ball to one player in area whose objective is to score by PUTTING FOOT ON THE BALL ON THE LINE behind opponent.
- Objective of defending player is to win ball and attack opposite line.
- Either player may slide tackle if necessary to prevent opponent from scoring.
- If ball goes out of bounds, coach immediately delivers another ball.
- Game ends with a "goal" or after one minute, whichever is sooner.
- Two new players enter game.
- Winning team is first to score five goals.

Player Objectives

DEFENDER
- To defend patiently, delaying forward progress of opponent and ball.
- To execute well-timed tackling.

ATTACKER
- To maintain possession of ball under pressure.

NOTE: This is an excellent game for 1 vs 1 dribbling.

Game Five

A 2 vs 2 game to encourage players to create shooting positions

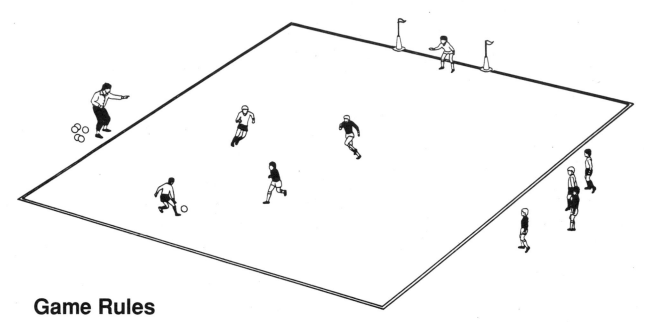

Game Rules

- 2 vs 2 (plus a goalkeeper) inside area 20 x 20 yards.
- Both teams try to score in same goal (six yards wide).
- When ball goes out of play, coach delivers another ball.
- If goalkeeper makes a save, ball goes to coach.
- After five balls are served, outfield players leave playing area, keeping score.
- Two more pairs enter area to compete, also keeping score.
- Score is ongoing and winner is team with more goals after 10 or 15 minutes.
- With large group of players (e.g., 16) half of players play small-sided game (4 vs 4) and then change groups.

Player Objectives

PLAYER WITH THE BALL:

- To manipulate ball to avoid challenges and to open up shooting positions.
- To keep head up to observe teammate, opponents and goal.
- To shoot when opportunity is there.
- To change direction — turn with ball.
- To shield ball where necessary.
- To change pace.

PLAYER WITHOUT THE BALL:

- To provide support for teammate.

Game Six

Practice to develop turning with the ball

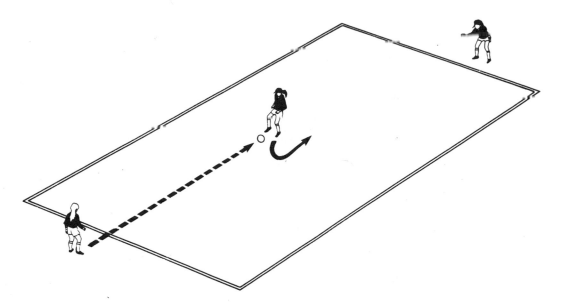

Game Rules

- Set up several identical areas, having groups of three players as shown.
- Each playing area is 10 x 20 yards.
- Play starts at one end.
- Ball is played to middle player who turns with ball and plays it to teammate.
- End player may control ball or play it first time back to middle player who turns and plays it to third player, with no more than two touches.
- End players must play ball from BEHIND respective lines.
- Each time ball returns to first end player, team scores one point: a point does not count if ball goes over sidelines, or if it is not played from BEHIND endlines.
- Winning team is first to score 20 points.
- Change middle player with one of end players and repeat game.

NOTE: A key to success is the middle player's ability to turn quickly.

Player Objectives

- To develop correct turning techniques.
- To achieve pace and accuracy in passing.

Game Seven

A 1 vs 1 game to develop correct shielding technique and passing opportunities from tight marking positions

Game Rules

- Set up game with four players, as shown, in area approximately 10 x 20 yards.
- Two players compete within area.
- Two players behind endlines may move along their respective lines to create a passing angle for middle player in possession of ball.
- Play starts with one of end players.
- Ball is played to one of middle players, whose objective is to play ball to OTHER end player.
- Opponent tries to win ball, ideally, to gain possession.
- Each time middle player "finds" an end player a goal is scored and possession is retained.
- Game is played for one minute: the winner is the player with the most goals.
- End players change with middle players and they compete to score goals.
- Winner is player to score most goals.

Player Objectives

- To be in position for ball.
- To control ball successfully.
- To shield ball from opponent.
- To be patient and not to give ball away unnecessarily.
- To create a passing angle.
- To achieve pace and accuracy in passing.

Game Eight

A 2 vs 2 game to encourage the wall pass

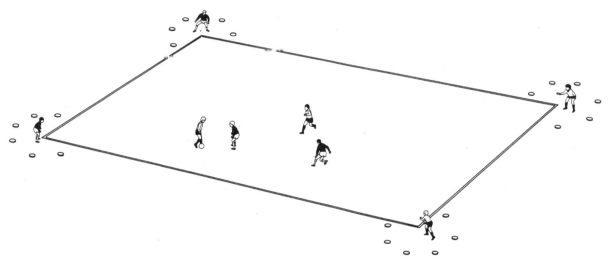

Game Rules

- Set up game with eight players in an area 20 x 30 yards.

- 2 vs 2 within area; other four players each stand on corner of area.

- Play starts with one of corner players who passes ball to one team. Each team must pass at least twice before playing to one of the corner target men within marked areas. If opponents win ball, they must do the same. Each successful target pass scores one point.

- Each successful wall pass scores 10 points. (for wall pass see page 54)

- Corner player returns pass to team playing ball to him.

- When ball goes out of bounds on the side, re-start play with kick-in from which wall pass can be used.

- Game is played for 2 minutes, then players change.

- Combined total of points should be kept; winning pair has more points after 10 – 15 minutes.

Player Objectives

- To achieve pace and accuracy in passing.

- To recognize wall pass.

- To execute wall pass.

NOTE: The same game may be used to encourage TAKEOVERS (see page 53) instead of the wall pass, or both actions may be encouraged.

Game Nine

A 2 vs 2 game to practice simple defending

Game Rules

- Set up the game in an area 20 x 30 yards with goals (three yards wide) but no goalkeepers.

- Players get in pairs and start at opposite endlines.

- Play starts when coach, at halfway line, plays ball towards one team; one pair from each team enters game.

- Both teams compete to score goals.

- If ball goes out of bounds or goal is scored, coach re-starts game with pass towards one team.

- After two minutes, two more opposing pairs enter game.

- Winner is team with more goals after 10 – 20 minutes.

Player Objectives

DEFENDING PLAYERS:

- To close down opponents quickly.
- To use the correct tackling technique.
- To " jockey" opponent correctly.
- To stay goalside of opponents.
- To time tackles.
- To provide defensive support.

NOTE: With a decreased area or an increased area, the game may be used for 1 vs 1 or 3 vs 3, respectively, with emphasis on correct defending.

Game Ten

The 4-a-side game to practice combining of players

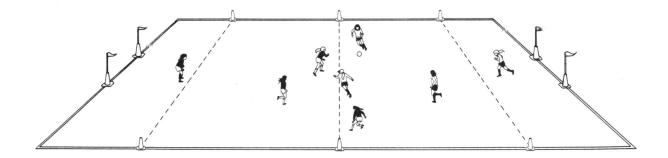

Game Rules

- Game is played in area 25 x 35 yards.

- Goals are five yards wide and five feet high (corner flag height).

- Halfway line and six-yard lines are marked; cones or markers define lines.

- Eight players maximum per team; four players within the area and four resting.

- Goalkeeper designated by each team may use hands only within six-yard area.

- Duration of each period three minutes; after game all players leave field and are replaced by resting teammates.*

- At end of second three minute game, original teams enter playing area; teams change ends and both teams must select a NEW goalkeeper.

- Game has corner kicks and throw-ins. Goal kicks must be taken within one yard of goal line and travel over six-yard line to be in field of play.

- After a goal, team conceding goal kicks off from center spot.

- Duration of game is decided by coach.

- Ongoing score may be kept; winning team is one to score most goals.

* Although the game is physically demanding, be aware "off the field" players are quickly rested and will become frustrated through inactivity. If in doubt, play two games simultaneously.

Player Objectives

OFFENSE:

- To combine successfully and score goals.

DEFENSE:

- To combine successfully and gain possession.

MASTERING TECHNIQUES

The Shape of Things to Come

Trying to master the techniques of soccer is a priority for players 9, 10 and 11 years of age. Not only should a principal emphasis in practice be technique work, but coaches should also encourage players to work on their own with the ball. The ages of 9, 10 and 11 are ideal for challenging technique practice. At that age, children have grown out of infant instability and are not yet encumbered by the awkwardness of their early teens.

Obviously the mechanics of performing specific techniques are important. In all cases, there are some basic considerations of which all players and coaches need to be aware — keeping an eye on the ball; and being aware of which part of the body strikes the ball are just two.

However, much has been written about the intricacies and subtleties of the mechanics of kicking and controlling. Over the years, coaches have had to suffer through such directions as the "non-kicking foot should be 10 inches from the ball, body leaning away, and allowing full extension of the leg and foot," etc., etc..... After painstaking study of the text, many coaches would be no better off — and frequently end up a little perplexed and frustrated after these kinds of directions.

Even experienced, successful professionals asked to describe, step-by-step, the process of executing a technique, would have extreme difficulty. However, if asked to perform the technique, some players would find the task simple. There is good reason for this; players learn technique through experience:
  • Observation of the technique performed by others;
  • Repetitive practice with and without the pressure of opposition;
  • Execution of the technique in games.

If a technique cannot be easily described, it stands to reason that it cannot be easily learned by verbal or written description. However, a technique can be better understood by observation of the "picture" which shows the SHAPE of the technique.

This section on techniques is a simpler and more effective way of teaching technique by looking at BODY SHAPE.

All good teachers know "a picture's worth a thousand words." But also "a picture tells the story."

The "body shape" tells of things to come. Bob McNab, the "former England and Arsenal great," now coaching in North America, was a left fullback who was naturally right-footed, but no one could tell. He would often say "pose for the camera" to get the "body shape" right for kicking the ball.

If you took a "picture" of a technically-sound soccer player just before kicking or receiving the ball, the "body shape" would tell you what was to come next — you could calculate what the chances were of performing the action successfully.

The arms, in particular — besides giving balance, provide a strong indicator of how the body is poised to perform a technique. In fact, a little attention to the arms and hands can greatly enchance the performance of techniques.

Nothing can beat a good demonstration. In the absence of a skilled demonstrator, a video is particularly effective because the technique is shown from the beginning to the end of the action. A video is even more helpful because the modern VCR allows for each stage in the execution of a technique to be "paused" and studied.

The illustrations in this chapter show examples of different techniques. Note the SHAPE created by the body, the head and the positions of the arms and legs. Each technique creates a unique **shape**.

What are the Key Techniques?

PASSING — Playing the ball with the feet. This is the most widely used of all techniques, and therefore, the most important to practice.

CONTROL — Receiving a ball, passed along the ground or in the air, using any part of the body to control the ball except the arms or hands.

HEADING — Playing aerial balls with the forehead.

TACKLING — Using the feet to win the ball and the body to correctly challenge for a ball in possession of an opponent.

DRIBBLING — Running with the ball and manipulating it with the feet.

SHOOTING — Trying to score by playing the ball with the feet or head, towards the opponents' goal.

Passing

Learning the technique of passing and applying it in game situations is a necessity for all young players.

SIDE FOOT PASS – Playing the ball along the ground with the inside (or the outside) of the foot is the most widely-used pass in the game. This technique is the easiest to learn and simplest to execute. The pass is used in all areas of the field and is effective over distances of five to 25 yards.

Position:
Body shaped to allow foot to turn out; a slight sitting-back posture to open hips; note arm positions.

LOW DRIVE – The execution of the low instep drive requires good timing and therefore much practice. A driven pass along the ground is an effective, quick method of changing play in a game. Low, driven crosses across the face of the opponents goal are also effective because they are difficult for opponents to counter. The most common and rewarding use for the low drive is when shooting the ball towards the opponents goal.

Position:
Head looking down; body and non-kicking knee flexed over the ball; arms and hands help "orchestrate" the movement.

LOFTED PASS – The lofted pass, where the ball is played through its underside with the lower instep (top of the big toe), is the most common crossing technique. It can be used effectively in all areas of the field to make aerial passes of over 25 yards.

Position:
    Body leaning away from the ball to open up the swing for the lofted kick — with full extension of leg and foot; arms loose, balancing the movement.

THE CHIP – The chip is a delicate aerial pass, played with the front of the foot (top of the toes) through the underside of the ball. This technique is designed to get the ball in the air quickly and drop it into the target area quickly; the backspin on the ball will also stop the ball quickly.

Position:
    Body hunched down, with head rounding downwards; arms are pulled down and locked on striking to enhance clipped action.

SWERVING PASS – The swerving pass is used to curl the ball in the air. The technique is effected by striking the ball through its lower center with the inside or outside of the foot, or by striking the lower outside of the ball directly with the instep.

This type of pass can be used in all areas of the field but is particularly effective at corner kicks, crossed balls and direct free kicks around the opponents' penalty area.

Coaching Points

Constant practice will improve the quality of passing techniques. However, the following coaching points should be taken into consideration when applying these techniques to the game itself.

1. WEIGHT OR PACE OF PASS – The pass should be played with the right amount of weight (pace) to either the feet of the receiver or the space into which the receiver is running, so that the receiver is able either to control the ball easily or play the ball comfortably with one touch.

2. ACCURACY – It is important that all passes are made accurately to "feet" or into "space."

3. TIMING OF THE PASS – The player in possession of the ball should not pass the ball if the intended receiver is not looking at the ball, is not yet ready, or is not moving into space to receive the ball comfortably. A poorly-timed pass often results in loss of possession of the ball.

4. TIMING OF THE RUN – The player making a run to receive a pass should ensure that the player in possession of the ball has the ball under good control, is ready to make the pass and is looking up and aware of his teammate. Not only is a poorly-timed run a waste of energy, but also it could result in a loss of possession.

5. SUPPORT – It is vital that the player in possession of the ball has immediate help from his teammates. The more options a player has to pass the ball, the easier it is for him to keep possession.

Control

When passing the ball, great care should be given to how the player receiving the ball is going to be able to control it. Good control is the means of maintaining possession and developing the team attack. Again, the shaping of the body in order to effect control of the ball is essential.

Methods of Control

 1 Chest – leaning back to cushion flighted pass; (introduce with gentle service).

 2. Thigh – raised to receive and control aerial passes.

 3. Instep – raised to control aerial passes.

 4. Side of foot – extended forward to receive and to control.

CUSHIONING

The first 4 methods of control use "cushioning" as the method of controlling the ball. The controlling surface is presented towards the ball and withdrawn on contact to take the pace off the ball.

 5. Sole of the foot – to wedge and push the ball into space.

 6. Inside and outside of foot – to wedge and drag the ball into space.

 7. Chest – leaning forward to control a ball which is bouncing off the ground.

TRAPPING/WEDGING

The final three methods of control make use of trapping and/or wedging. Part of the body is used to wedge or trap the ball between the ground and the controlling surface of the body.

Coaching Points

1. Make an early selection in method.

2. Get in line with the flight of the ball.

3. Keep the eyes on the ball.

4. a) Relax the controlling surface or,
   b) Wedge the ball.

5. Pass the ball accurately or keep possession.

Indecision Leads to Poor Control

Many mistakes in control are caused by indecision, the player failing to make an early selection of the method of control. Often this results in the player being upright at the moment of control. The ball rebounds off the body instead of hitting it like a cushion. There is a "body shape" to each method of control. Observe the illustrations and note that the players' bodies are never upright at the moment of control.

Heading

Heading should not be regarded as a principal technique for players 9, 10 and 11 years of age. Guided by recent medical evidence, we are concerned that heading during this age period should be introduced slowly and with gentle service (see related information in appendix and related game on page 26).

Shooting

Shooting is the most rewarding of all the techniques, but for many players, the most difficult. There is a great temptation for players to look up at the goal as they are about to kick the ball. The techniques for shooting with the feet are almost identical to passing, other than the volley and half-volley.

Techniques

1) Side foot.
2) Low drive – instep.
3) Swerve shot – inside and outside of foot.
4) Volley – is a shot taken with the ball in the air with the need to keep the ball inside the goalposts and under the cross bar, ideally dipping downwards to maximize the difficulty for the goalkeeper.
5) Half-volley – takes place when a shot is taken just as an aerial ball strikes the ground. This ball has to be kept under the height of the cross bar. The ground half-volley usually causes the greatest difficulty for the goalkeeper.

VOLLEY SHOT

Volley and Half-volley kicking occurs only rarely in play outside the penalty boxes. It is such an important method of scoring that situations presenting the opportunity for this type of shooting should be frequently used in practice (see page 46).

Coaching Points

1) The same principles apply to shooting as to individual passing techniques.
2) It is important that players look at the ball during the whole process of striking the ball.
3) Players should ensure that their ankles are locked as they are about to strike the ball.
4) Players must be prepared to withstand a physical challenge as they prepare to shoot and therefore may need to modify their body shape accordingly (see related game on page 28).

Tackling

Well-timed tackling is an important defensive "weapon" for any team. It is vital that coaches stress that their players TACKLE THE BALL and not their opponents. Not only is it a foul to tackle an opponent, but also it could cause unnecessary injury. However, the body can and should be used — fairly — to assist the tackle. CHALLENGE FAIRLY WITH THE BODY — WIN THE BALL WITH THE FEET.

Although tackling should be introduced at ages 9, 10 and 11, greater emphasis on this vital aspect of the game should occur during the early teens. However, it is important that players learn to defend in 1 vs 1 situations (see pages 56 and 57 for more information, and related game on page 27).

Dribbling

WHAT IS DRIBBLING?

1) Running with the ball at feet.
2) Manipulating and faking with the ball.
3) Moving the ball past opponents.
4) Shielding the ball.

Coaching Points

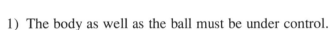

1) The body as well as the ball must be under control.
2) Manipulation of the ball to throw opponents off balance.
3) Movement of the body to throw opponents off balance.
4) Change of pace.
5) Change of direction.
6) Sideways stance of the body (shielding).
7) Body between the ball and the opponent.
8) Turning away from the opponent.
(See related game on page 30).

Summary

All technique practices, however simple, SHOULD EXCITE THE IMAGINATION OF THE PLAYERS by being in the form of a COMPETITION. Mundane, static, unchallenging technique drills will lead to boredom, a lack of interest and, ultimately, bad habits.

The technique practices described in the Howe Way provide examples of simple games, that call for repetition of technique but which challenge the players to improve performance.

THE WAITERSWAY

We have continually stressed in this book that young soccer players need fun and activity; children need to PLAY; and the "game is the teacher."

TONY WAITERS

The practices and games that follow are proven. They work. The children have fun. Most of the games are acceptable to players of all ages — pros included — but have been selected for this manual because of their particular relevance to 9, 10 and 11 year olds.

In many parts of the world, there is no organized soccer for players under the age of 12. But in most countries soccer is the national sport. It has high visibility and status nationally and within each community. Where there is no organized soccer, children "organize" themselves — and they play.

In North America, soccer has to be organized and somewhat structured — although the message should remain the same. But although children are organized, they should have plenty of opportunity to play. Winning or losing is not important. That each player has the opportunity to score is important. Let players express themselves. Let them experiment.

Above all, LET THEM PLAY.

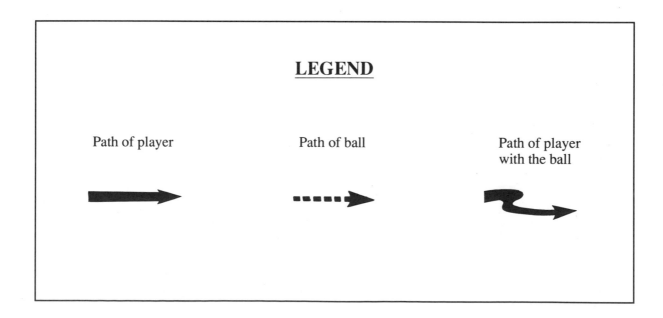

LEGEND

Path of player

Path of ball

Path of player with the ball

Micro Soccer

Objective

To give each player plenty of opportunity to kick the ball in a 3 vs 3 game and to gain a fundamental understanding of the game of soccer.

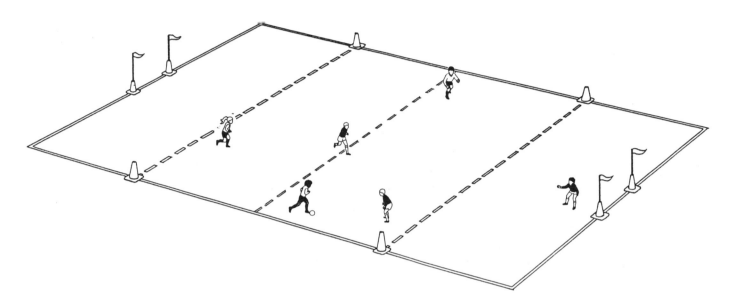

Organization

- Field size 20 x 30 yards.

- Six-yard "boxes" within which designated goalkeeper may handle — marked by cones or lines.

- Center line marked by cones/lines.

- Each player takes a turn in goal, for three minutes.

- When ball goes out of play, game is re-started by:
  Sideline – throw-in (or pass-in)
  Endline – goal kick or corner kick depending on which player last touched ball.

- After a goal re-start with either goal kick or center kick (if center — opponents must retreat to own six-yard line).

- In practice with numbers greater than six, either have two 3 vs 3, or if less than 12, have separate practice operating and rotate players in and out of the 3 vs 3 game.

Coaching Points

- Encourage at least one player to go fully wide on goal kicks or when goalkeeper has ball in hands.

- Encourage goalkeeper to move off line to support attacks or to intercept through balls.

- Encourage players to pass, dribble and communicate with each other.

- On throw-ins, encourage non-throwing attacker to look for a forward shooting chance — and not to go too close to thrower.

Challenge

- To outscore opposition.

The Zone Game

Objective

To develop combined offensive and defensive play in a 3 vs 3 game.

Organization

- Area 30 x 20 yards, with additional five yard zones at each end.

- Normal 3 vs 3 but the only way to score is by "touch down" of ball with foot in end zone.

- If ball goes out of play over end zone line or at side of end zone, game re-started by defending team with "goal kick" or "dribble-in" from endline.

- If ball goes out over side line (not including end zone) play is re-started by "pass-in" (or throw-in if coach prefers).

- Condition game to disallow any slide tackling.

Coaching Points

- The only way to score is by dribbling or passing into end zone — both methods should be encouraged.

- Player attempting to score should screen ball from opponent as **he/she** "touches down" — both to protect ball and player.

- Defending team must work collectively to stop "dribbler" and at same time avoid being "blindsided" by pass.

Challenge

- To outscore opposition.

The Four-Goal Game

Objective

To encourage "composure" on-the-ball, "awareness of teammates" and team cooperation.

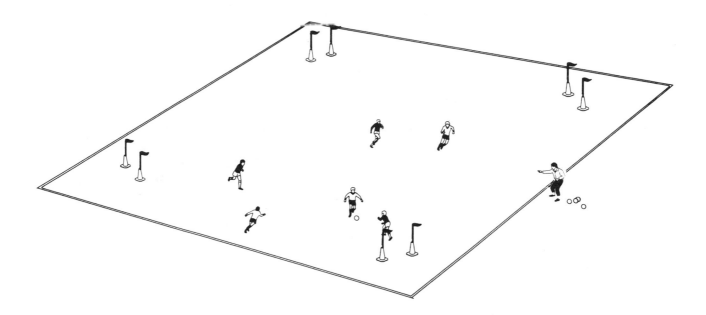

Organization

- Area 30 x 30 yards.

- Four goals are set-up by cones or markers five yards out from each corner. Goals are one yard wide.

- Three players in possession combine to score in any of the four goals.

- They can only score through front of goal and may dribble or pass through goal and still maintain possession.

- When ball goes out of play, re-start with either a throw-in or pass-in.

Coaching Points

- Encourage players to "switch" the play by passing, as three defending players can quickly mark three out of the four goals.

- Encourage players to turn away with ball if one goal becomes "marked" by opponent.

- If attacking teams are not having success, consider giving them a further option. Let the team in possession also score a "goal" by getting four consecutive passes.

Challenge

- To outscore the opposition.

- (If the 4 Pass scoring rule is also being used, the **challenge** for the coach is to keep the score — and count the passes!).

Chip 'n Dale

Objective

To develop in a 3 vs 3 game, attacking cooperation and chipping techniques and good collective defending positions relative to attackers.

Organization

- Area 35 x 25 yards

- Mark ½ circle zone at ends.

- 3 vs 3, with team in possession attempting to chip ball into hands of teammates in zone.

- To score, ball cannot bounce before reaching zone; ball must be caught by player in zone without catcher stepping outside.

- Coach serves balls, and changes players from zone to field every three or four minutes.

Coaching Points

- Attackers have to create angle or space to be able to chip successfully.

- Passing/dribbling/faking are methods to create opening for chipped "shot".

- Defenders must send one man to hustle player with ball to prevent easy chip.

- Other defenders must correctly support hustler to prevent pass giving clear chance for attacker to chip.

Challenge

- To outhustle and outscore opposition.

Criss-Cross

Objective

To allow all players the opportunity of experiencing the goalkeeping role — in catching high balls and as an introduction to cross ball situations.

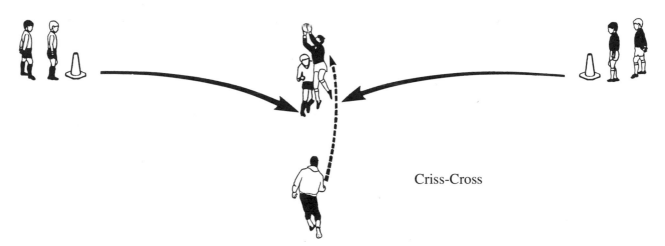

Criss-Cross

Organization

- Whenever possible work with two groups.

- Use "Catch and Hug" as part of the warm-up. Players, five yards apart, throw to each other.

- In Criss-Cross, catchers come from one marker; attackers from the other; and change places.

- Attackers are not allowed to physically challenge for ball.

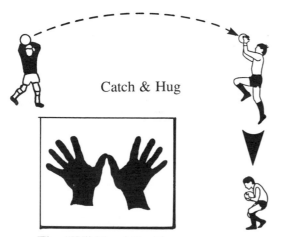

Catch & Hug

The "W" Hand Position

Coaching Points

- When catching high balls, form a "W" with thumbs and index fingers (see illustration).

- In both introductory and crossing practice as players shape to catch ball, palms should be facing ball: arms forward and reaching but comfortable.

- In "Catch and Hug" after the "Catch", let ball drop into body for the "Hug".

- In Criss-Cross, body should be in half-turned position — towards ball and opponent.

- Whenever possible the "catcher" should take ball in front of attacker, i.e.... in relation to server.

- Whenever possible, "catcher" should take ball at highest "comfortable" position, ie.... not at full stretch, arms slightly flexed at elbows.

Challenge

- To catch ball cleanly and secure it.

Side Kicks

Objective

To introduce crossing from the side of the goals and to convert cross balls by accurate shooting, plus goalkeeping experience for all players.

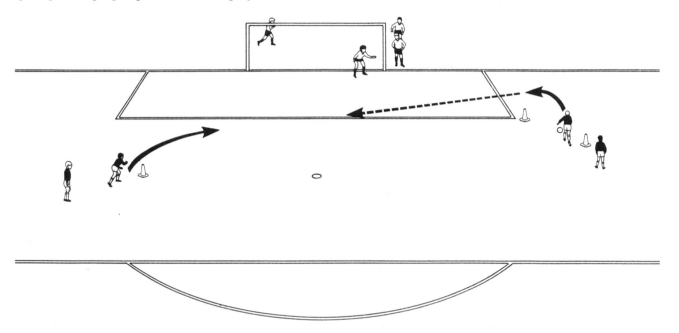

Organization

- Use existing field with goals or improvise area with cones, markers and corner flags.

- Split group into two even teams.

- One team "attacks," the other "defends" as goalkeepers.

- Crossing players start from rear cone — take ball forward and must cross over beyond second cone.

- Goalkeeper must stand at near post — otherwise crossers can shoot.

- Ball is "crossed" to teammate who moves from "far post area" cone to shoot — one touch only.

- "Defenders" take turns in goal by rotating after each cross.

- Attacking players alternate from crossing file to shooting file.

Coaching Points

- Low ground cross easier to convert than high ball, other than for heading.

- Goalkeeper be alert for slow cross — go out and intercept — but without anticipating.

- Accuracy of shot usually more important than power.

- Shooter at far cone should time run and not move off cone too early.

- Goalkeeper should move from near post across the goal — face shot and "stay big."

Challenge

- Each team gets set number of attacks (eg. 20) — team that scores the most wins. Good goalkeeping keeps the score down.

Through Balls

Objective

To teach all players the correct technique when a goalkeeper dives at the feet of onrushing opponent — and thus help avoid one of the most serious injury-threatening situations in youth soccer.

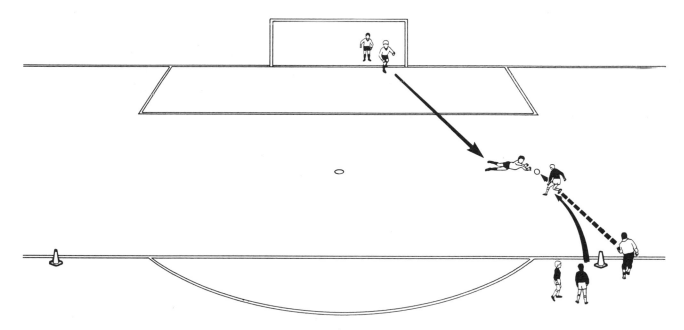

Organization

- Use existing goal and penalty area when available — if not, improvise with cones and markers.

- Try to keep to maximum of six players per practice group.

- Coach acts as server and rolls ball to give realistic service slightly in favour of goalkeeper.

- Goalkeepers should start in correct position — covering near post just off the goal line. They cannot move until ball is rolled.

- Attacker is not allowed to kick ball or physically challenge for ball (to avoid injury risk).

- Rotation from attacking file to goalkeeping file.

- After five to seven minutes, change angle of approach from right side of goal to left side.

Coaching Points

- Goalkeepers should move to ball quickly with low crouching run.

- Slide rather than dive to side diving position.

- Hands should go to ball with the head covering near post and body and legs covering across goal and the far post.

- When "diving", stay on the side — not stomach — with body parallel to goal line.

- Once ball is secured — pull into body and wrap body around ball.

Challenge

- To secure ball cleanly with good technique.

The Three-Shot Stop

Objective

A goalkeeping diving practice for all players, involving reaction work, side-diving technique and "recovery."

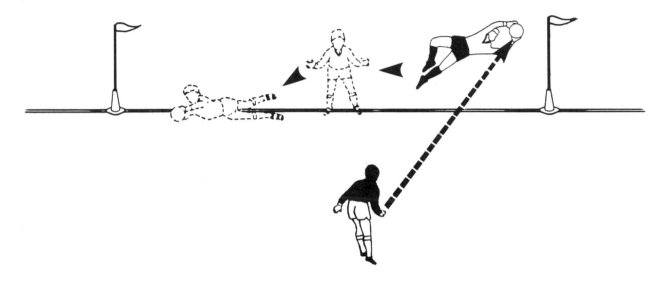

Organization

- Work in pairs. If odd number, have one group of three or spare player with coach.

- Improvise goals approximately six yards wide.

- One player with a ball (preferably two) faces "goalkeeper" and serves an easy shot by hand.

- Goalkeeper must dive for ball and begin to throw ball back to server while on ground, while at same time recovering to feet.

- Server gives just enough time for goalkeeper to recover before serving second ball.

- Server must not "fake" when serving.

- Server should vary type of service — ground save, aerial save, simulated header downwards, etc.

- "Goalkeepers" change after three shots.

Coaching Points

- Dive on side — not on stomach. Do not roll on back — imperative if goalkeeper is to be able to recover quickly to feet.

- Ball is thrown back from "open" position. The "throw" movement should be used to give momentum to aid recovery to feet.

Challenge

- To save and recover quickly while maintaining "side" and open position.

Noah's Lark (2 by 2)

Objective

To combine in attack and defense in a challenging game with two players on each side.

Organization

- Area 30 x 20 yards area with goals eight yards wide.

- 6 vs 6 — with partners assigned on each team: each partner given a number 1 to 3.

- Coach shouts number (1–3) and rolls ball into play.

- The two pairs with that number come out of goal to compete against each other.

- Remaining players must stay on goal line and defend goal without using hands.

- Goals can only be scored below knee height.

- When ball goes out of play, coach can immediately serve in another to same pairs — or allow pairs to go back to goal line.

- Ball can be played back to "goalkeepers," who must play ball back after no more than two touches.

- Do not let "goalkeepers" move out off goal line. Penalty kick from six yards out if they do.

Coaching Points

- When defending, one player should go to player with ball.

- Supporting player must watch other attacker, mark the dangerous space and cover partner (see page 58) all at the same time.

- Coach should encourage dribbling, passing and shooting to the "team" in possession.

- See sections on techniques (page 34) and skills (page 51).

- Encourage "goalkeepers" to defend as a wall together and to move as a unit to block shooting angle.

Challenge

- One team vs the other, also pairs to keep a count of goals scored and conceded.

Square Pegs

Objective

To improve "touch" on the ball (ball control) and to practice carefully-weighted chip volleys.

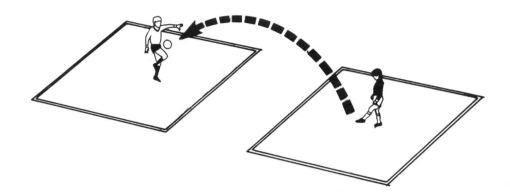

Organization

- Using markers/grids, organize six-yard squares four yards apart.

- To start practice, one player bounces ball by hand and volleys to partner in opposite square.

- Organize squares to accommodate all players at practice. If odd number, rotate the third player among the pairs.

- Player in square can have as many touches as desired but ball can bounce only once before being returned.

- Adjust size and distance of areas to ability of players (if necessary, allow two bounces in square).

Coaching Points

- Don't juggle the ball. "First touch" on receiving ball should set-up ball for return volley.

- Try to make flight and weight of pass to give most considerate service to partner for control of ball.

- Give pass some height to allow partner time to adjust.

- Use chest and thigh whenever possible to set up return volley.

Challenge

- Which pair can make the highest number of consecutive passes.

THE AGE OF SKILL

As players graduate from the beginner phase into the "Golden Age" they become very capable of progressing from the basic skills they have already learned — particularly those skills of dribbling, passing and ball control. These young players are ready and willing to enhance their play by adding some exciting intricacies.

The next segment will present some of these possibilities — mainly from a creative attacking viewpoint, and we would strongly recommend that all coaches of "the Golden Age" players should study the next seven pages.

However, coaches should not feel they must go out on the practice field and develop all of these more involved skills with the players. Nevertheless, experimentation by the players should always be encouraged — particularly if a mistake has resulted.

If the coach feels confident in "showing" how the skill can be acquired or applied, then by all means "coach the play." If unsure, the coach should not worry but continue to encourage experimentation by the players and let the practices and the games be the teacher.

Individual Possession

Modern soccer has placed a heavy emphasis on passing the ball as means of possession. While this is important, many coaches destroy individual creativity and dribbling ability in the process.

The art of good coaching is to help players recognize when to pass the ball and when to keep it.

The illustrations in this chapter demonstrate a few of the many moves a player may practice to keep possession.

Turning with the ball —without close marking

There are times in a game when a player has
    1) time and room to turn with the ball
    2) to change direction
    3) or to change the direction of the ball.

The illustrations show three methods of turning with the ball. The method is dictated by where the ball is received and by the situation of the opponent. In all these examples, the ball is received on the right side of the player's body. In all, the player moves towards the ball before turning.

Illustration 1 — No opponent in the vicinity. Player's weight is on left foot. Player pushes the INSIDE of the right foot towards the ball just before impact. Player "cushions" the ball by withdrawing right foot with the ball and turning to the right. This technique produces a tight turn and sets the player up to dribble or pass with either foot.

Illustration 1

Illustration 2 — Before receiving the ball, the player observes an opponent on the left side, not too close. So the player turns to the right, and away from the opponent. The advantage of using the OUTSIDE of the right foot to execute the turn is that this technique moves the ball away from the opponent and sets the player up in stride for the next step.

Illustration 2

Illustration 3 — Having already observed the opponent on the right, the player turns the ball left and away from the opponent, with the inside of right foot. Turning with the ball on the right, the player keeps between the ball and the opponent. (see related game on page 29).

Illustration 3

Turning with the ball – against tight marking

In a 1 vs 1 situation, the player in possession has to decide whether to pass or to take on the opponent. If it's the latter, HOW does the player beat the opponent? This decision is dictated by the opponent's position, and the available space on the opponent's goal side, the area behind the opponent.

In the illustration, the opponent is goal side of the player with the ball. The tight marking position of the opponent is denying the space, but there is space behind the defender. By turning the right foot towards the ball, the player "opens up" the stance and is able to spin taking the ball with the left foot in

the direction shown. It is important that the player with the ball TURNS AWAY from an opponent to avoid giving the defender a chance to tackle (see related game on page 30).

Faking and accelerating — against tight marking

In recent years more and more players with outstanding control have been performing excellent faking or hesitation moves. However, too often those moves have been executed too far in front of an opponent and, therefore, totally wasted. The fake may look good, but only serves to alert the defender to the attacker's fancy footwork.

The idea of a fake is to get the opponent unbalanced or wrong-footed. It must be performed close enough to the opponent that the opponent can't recover.

In the illustration below, the opponent has been caught on the 'wrong-side' of the attacker, (i.e. not goal side) but is running back and is quickly gaining. The attacking player with the ball hesitates over the ball by performing a little hop on the left foot and moving the right foot around the ball ONCE. At the beginning of the second rotation, the ball is played forward and the player accelerates. The movement of the foot around the OUTSIDE of the ball allows the player to play the ball immediately in the right direction; the little hop sets the player immediately in stride. But the main purpose of the fake is to make the opponent hesitate long enough for the player with the ball to accelerate into the space.

Both examples in this chapter show the player with the ball penetrating the defensive position by identifying WHERE THE SPACE IS ON THE GOAL SIDE of the defender and attacking that space. (see related games on pages 30 and 42).

Combining to Keep Possession

In their early soccer years, from ages 5 – 7, players are "selfish." This is natural. Until the age of 5, children usually play alone or with a friend. They are not used to sharing.

When they start to play soccer in any type of game situation there is only one "toy" — the ball. Therefore it is natural to see the "swarm" effect in games played by young children. THEY ALL WANT TO PLAY WITH THE BALL AT THE SAME TIME and when they get it, they do not want to share it, nor do they know how.

Children aren't born with social skills. Yet they have to "socialize" in team play. The process of interacting is developed through experience.

At ages 9, 10 and 11 players begin to recognize the advantage of sharing the ball to keep possession. As coaches, we can provide this experience by putting players into realistic situations that will help them to see the "pictures" that the game presents and to recognize "what is on" for them to do in the game.

This chapter describes simple combination plays, their recognition and their execution.

Support

The more support a player has from teammates, the more options the player has with the ball. The "picture" that the game presents will help the player make the decision to pass the ball or keep it.

In illustrations 1 and 2, the attacking players are trying to combine to keep possession against one defending player.

In illustration 1, the player with the ball has only one real option and that is to keep the ball because the teammate is "hiding" behind an opponent. In this situation, it is impossible to play the ball directly to the feet of the teammate.

In illustration 2, the teammate has moved "into an open space" on the field to be "seen" by a teammate and to present a passing opportunity for the player with the ball. This support gives the player in possession two options — to keep the ball or to pass it (see related game on pages 24 and 43).

Takeover

A takeover occurs when two players, moving from opposite directions, pass by each other, one of the players dribbling the ball. The player with the ball can keep the ball or leave it for a teammate as the teammate passes by. A successful takeover occurs under these conditions:
  1) The two players must move towards each other (see illustration on next page).
  2) The player with the ball must not move it to the other foot, or change the "line" of the ball.
  3) The player must keep the body between the ball and the opponent.
  4) The teammate passes by, at speed, expecting to take the ball.
  5) If the dribbler "leaves" the ball, it must be <u>left</u>, not touched as the teammate passes by.

There are times when the ball may be kept, where the dribbler would elect to keep the ball and go 1-on-1 to attack the space behind.

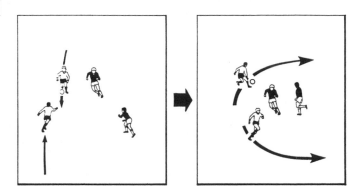

REMEMBER

• The player with the ball always makes the DECISION TO KEEP OR LEAVE THE BALL.

• If the ball is dribbled on the right foot, it will be taken over with the right foot of the player passing by.

• VERBAL COMMUNICATION IS NOT NECESSARY. If the teammates talk, they alert their opponents to the takeover.

The takeover is an excellent combination play to change the direction of play or to create space against tight marking opponents — it should be encouraged and practiced — first in pairs then in a related game. Don't be too critical if they try — and fail. It requires practice and understanding (see related games on pages 28 and 42).

Wall Pass

The wall pass occurs when two players (one with the ball) position themselves in positions similar to the one shown on the illustration. Timing and technique are key factors in the success.

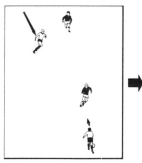 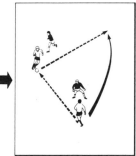

The illustration shows a typical example of a wall pass opportunity. Successful execution will penetrate the positions of the defenders and will occur under the following conditions:

1) The attacking player with the ball must commit opponent by dribbling towards the defending player.

2) The ball must be passed at a distance not so far that it will give the opponent time to recover defensively, but not so close that the opponent is able to make a tackle or intercept the pass.

3) The ball must be passed with the FRONT FOOT (the foot nearer to the opponent). The direction of the pass is to a point between the feet of a teammate. This gives the teammate two options to use either foot to return the pass. The pass must be well paced.

4) The dribbler/passer must accelerate immediately after the pass.

5) The support player, "the wall," must move to keep "inside" the rear defending player. The timing in making that move is key to success.

6) The "wall" player must adopt an "open stance" to both see to pass the ball and view the marker at the same time...45° is a good guideline. That stance also makes the execution of the return pass easier, again accurately into the path of the teammate.

While the support player must recognize the wall pass opportunity, the DECISION to execute the play is made by the PLAYER WITH THE BALL. Instead of passing the ball, the player may try to dribble it past an opponent.

The support player receiving the ball makes the decision whether or not to return the pass. For example, if an opponent is too tight the receiver may elect to turn with the ball (refer to illustration on previous page).

The intention of the wall pass is to penetrate one or more opponents. While it may be used in midfield, it's particularly effective in the final third of the field. (See related games on pages 31, 42 and 43).

Third Man Running

As players become more experienced, they begin to understand their movements in relation to the dictates of the game. As they develop as players, they begin to see "what is on."

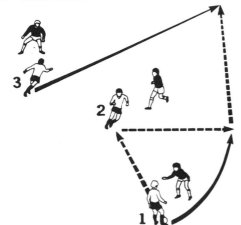

In this segment, the co-operation between two players and their VISUAL COMMUNICATION has been discussed. Now a THIRD player enters the picture. The concept of Third Man Running has already been described in the earlier section "The Game is the Teacher."

The attacking player in possession (player 1) combines with the teammate (player 2) as shown. Attacking player 3 could receive the next pass from player 1 and make a penetrating run, as shown.

ACCURACY and **PACE OF PASS** plus the **TIMING OF THE RUN** of the third player are the keys to success.

Player 3 must start run just as the ball is leaving the feet of player 2. This will give player 1 time to SEE THE RUN and MAKE THE PASS.

Assume that the defender marking attacking player 3 is a good player and remains "goal side" of the opponent. At the very least, the attacking team will maintain possession and the positions of the other two defenders will have been penetrated.

Note: Introduction to Third Man Running. Coaches should introduce this combination play in a warm-up WITHOUT OPPOSITION so that players begin to understand its concept without the interference of opponents.

Summary

When a team gains or regains possession of the ball, the players are not generally within shooting distance of their opponent's goal. There are only two ways of progressing to the shooting zone while mastering control of the ball:
1) Dribbling
2) Passing.

Even the world's greatest dribblers are hard pressed to beat four or five players on a run towards the shooting zone. Possession is the key to success. The combinations described in this chapter detail the option either to dribble or pass. There are several crucial points:
1) To recognize "what is on"
2) To play "what you see"
3) To avoid giving the ball away

Practice is the key to success. In time, players will execute the movements with flair, and precision and their actions will be unpredictable.

SIMPLE DEFENDING

One of the attractive aspects of soccer is that all players have the opportunity to play both offense and defense. Indeed, they MUST play both offense and defense. Soccer is a two-way game, going forward to attack and recovering to defend.

Coaches of players 9, 10 and 11 years of age must recognize the importance of working on both aspects in practice. As it is much more difficult to create than to destroy, more practice time should be devoted to the players' understanding of offensive principles and functions and to mastering the techniques of the game. However, it would be A MISTAKE TO NEGLECT DEFENSE.

Of every six practice sessions, FIVE should be devoted to offense and ONE to defense.

This chapter discusses simple defending.

1 vs 1

1 vs 1 is the simplest tactical situation in a game. The decisions and questions for both offensive and defensive players are clear.

On offense: "Can I take my player on, can I pass the ball, or should I protect the ball and wait for help?"

On defense: "Can I win the ball or should I delay my opponent and make it difficult for him to pass the ball forward?"

While the questions are simple, the execution is more difficult.

Much of the defender's work can be accomplished BEFORE the opponent receives the ball, by closing the distance between them WHILE THE BALL IS EN ROUTE. In order of priority, the defender should first consider intercepting the pass, then closing down the opponent before there's time to turn with the ball, and if the opponent has turned, trying to delay the forward progress of the ball.

With experience, anticipation and skillful marking, good players will be able to intercept some passes. Naturally, that saves them work. However, there are many situations where the ball cannot be intercepted and patient defending is required.

In illustration 1, the attacking player is in possession of the ball but with his back to the opponent's goal and the defender.

The defender should be far enough from the attacking player to see the ball. Otherwise, the opponent with the ball may spin and go past. Nor should the defender be so far away from the opponent that the attacking player is able to turn without pressure and face the defender with the ball.

Illustration 1

While size and ability dictate the exact defensive position, a good guide to the distance a defender should be from an opponent is an arm's length. Therefore, by extending an arm (slightly bent) the defender would be able to touch the opponent. Naturally, the defender should not actually touch the player as this may constitute a foul.

PATIENCE is the key to success. The defender CANNOT win the ball in this situation. To try will almost certainly result in a foul (tackling from behind). While the ball is in this position the defending player is not in danger.

The defender should attempt to win the ball only when the opponent tries to turn with the ball. The defender must TACKLE THE BALL and NOT THE OPPONENT, focussing attention on the ball at all times and not being thrown off balance by the movement of opponent's body.

If the attacking player elects to pass the ball, the defender's FIRST PRIORITY is to REMAIN on the defending GOALSIDE OF THE OPPONENT.

Illustration 2

In illustration 2, the attacking player is in possession of the ball and facing the defender and the opponent's goal.

The position adopted by the defending player is goalside of opponent. A sideways, "open" stance is best, at a 45-degree angle to the player, who is forced to the outside. This position has several advantages.

1) It prevents the attacking player from dribbling or passing the ball inside the defender.

2) It dictates to the opponent the direction that the defender wants the attacking player to go.

3) It gives the defender the chance to turn quickly. Knees are slightly flexed and weight is on the front foot (nearer to the opponent), allowing defender to push off when required.

4) It also sets the defender up to challenge at the right opportunity.

The defender in this role is like a tiger stalking prey, always alert yet relaxed, waiting to pounce. The challenge should be quick and strong.

The coach should explain to the team how their timing is essential to a successful challenge:

- Don't "dive in" to ball when unsure of result.

- Be patient.

- Tackle with resolve.

- Tackle when you know the ball can be won.

(See related game on page 27).

2 vs 2

In the same way that players on offense combine to keep possession, on defense they combine to win back the ball.

In the illustration, defender 1 is playing 1 vs 1 against the immediate opponent, with responsibilities as described on the previous page. The defender's only function is to focus on the opponent and the ball.

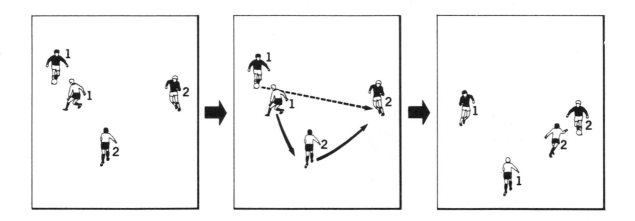

Defender 2 can afford to perform more than one function — almost taking a half and half position. Half marking — half covering.

Defender 2 takes a position in support of teammate, adopting an "open" stance to see the ball and opponent (attacker 2) at the same time. Position is goalside of opponent and the line is always closer to the ball than the opponent.

From the support or cover position, defender 2 is able to move across to delay attacker 1 if defender 1 is beaten. The support position also makes it difficult for attacker 1 to play a through pass.

If attacking player 1 passes the ball to attacking player 2, defender 2 closes in quickly to "jockey" opponent. DEFENDER 1 MUST IMMEDIATELY DROP BACK TO SUPPORT. It is important to note that most defenders, will want to follow the ball in this situation. This is a common mistake because the ball is like a magnet. Good practice and good coaching information help to cure players of this bad habit (see related games on pages 32 and 49).

Summary

In the history of the game, all great teams have been able to maintain possession of the ball under pressure, plus they have had the determination and produced the effort and skill to win the ball back.

APPENDIX

The Game is the Teacher

Does it teach two-footedness?

The one ongoing emphasis throughout this manual has been that "The Game is the Teacher." It is vital to put children in game situations and let them play. We will continue to beat that drum — forever!

However, you will probably have noticed small contradictions. Some recommended practices have been heavily structured in order to emphasize certain skills, and therefore are more like "drills."

It is not always possible for the game to be the teacher. Why? The simple reason is that in a game the player makes the decisions. The player may decide not to head the ball or not to kick and pass with the left foot.

We have already recommended a gradual, gentle development of heading skills — with the main emphasis on heading development coming later (the early teens onwards). But a two-footed player is admired the world over — and is always a more complete player.

Without doubt, the years between 6 and 12 are the most important in developing "Two-Footedness" and practices should be structured to encourage the development of this "skill."

Coaching Through the Kids' Eyes

There is an expression among professional coaches that "you coach through your own eyes." From the coach's eyes and brain and lips comes the experience influenced by background and environment — including beliefs and biases!

The more an adult has been steeped in the traditions of soccer, the more that person as a coach is likely to present the game the way he or she thinks it should be played.

Thus, an ex-Brit coaching in North America may present an English or Scottish soccer perspective and may impose a certain style of play. In the same way, coaches who were Scandinavian or Brazilian, Yugoslav or Russian would have a tendency to "coach through their own eyes" — as influenced by their upbringing.

The parent coach brought up in a non-traditional soccer environment may feel disadvantaged when taking the coaching responsibility — because of a lack of knowledge, experience and background. This "new" soccer person may, in fact, have some advantages over the "traditionalist."

Coaching youngsters from 6 – 12 should be accomplished "through the children's eyes." How do they view the game? What do they want from soccer?

If we ask ourselves those two questions — on a regular basis — instead of assuming we know what is the best for children, then we may all do a better job. Our young players want fun, kicks of the ball, activity and a place on the team.

At this age they will not be overly concerned about winning and losing, about having a set position, or about tactical formations. Those aspects of the game — important as they are — should come later.

Organization of the Practice

The Coaching Function is a numbers game.

- How many coaches/assistants/helpers are there?
- How many players are there?
- How many balls are there?

Those three numbers will determine the nature and quality of the practice and how it is to be organized.

It is very important that the players are active, and they should not be still for extended periods. They should be allowed to play "freely" for a sizeable portion of the session.

A shortage of helpers and soccer balls, plus large numbers of players at practice, will present a testing situation if certain objectives (fun, activity, skills development) are to be achieved. These objectives may still be achieved but with greater difficulty.

For instance, with large numbers, split the group into three teams (12 = 3 teams of 4; 15 = 3 teams of 5). Don't be overly concerned if you find you have uneven numbers (11, 13, 14 won't split perfectly).

Set up two practice areas.

This allows two teams to play while the third team has a 5 – 7 minute skills game or practice. By rotating the teams, each one plays the others and everyone has the opportunity of developing skills in the practice.

Even without an assistant, a 4-a-side game will continue without close supervision, allowing the coach to concentrate on the "skills group."

Marking out two small fields will also give the flexibility later to form four teams for a 3-a-side or 4-a-side mini-tournament to finish the session.

It is not recommended that a coach accept a situation where there will be no assistance and few soccer balls. But realistically some coaches will have to operate in these circumstances.

Why 3-a-side? Why 4-a-side?

Since the first Howe/Waiters manual "Coaching 6, 7 and 8 Year Olds," readers have asked the same question. "Why coach 3-a-side soccer when in games we play 6-a-side (or 5-a-side or 7-a-side)?"

We expect the same concern with our recommendation of 4-a-side as the base game for 9, 10 and 11 year olds. "Why practice 4-a-side when we play 7-a-side (or 8-a-side or 11-a-side)?"

The best answer is provided by the professional soccer players who rarely practice in 11-a-side. Small-sided games are the daily diet of the pros. Small-sided games provide the ideal learning situation for uncomplicated (in terms of numbers) practice in the vital phases and aspects of the game.

Soccer is played the world over in triangles — in threes! Often, the entire progression from the defensive end of the field into the final attacking area (penalty area) in 11-a-side play is effected by 3 players — with the remaining eight either as secondary support, or as decoys, or positioning themselves for the final pass or cross that creates the scoring chance.

At the end of almost every practice session, professional coaches give the players their "treat" — a scrimmage! What do the players chose to play? 11-a-side? Never! They play 6, 7 or 8-a-side games everytime! More involvement! More kicks of the ball! More fun!

	PRACTICE GAME	MATCH PLAY
6, 7 and 8 Year Olds	3 vs 3	3 vs 3 — 5 vs 5
9, 10 and 11 Year Olds	4 vs 4	7 vs 7 — 11 vs 11
The pros	7 vs 7	11 vs 11

Social Groups

In the first book "Coaching 6, 7 and 8 Year Olds," we discussed sociological groupings in relation to the ages of children.

It is known, for instance, that most 6 and 7 year olds have a special friend, and do not often socialize in groups of more than three (3-a-side soccer). Later, (9, 10 and 11), they become more social and are more prepared to co-operate and share, but still do not normally choose to work in large groups (4-a-side soccer). The "gang" concept (11-a-side) comes later — as boys and girls become teenagers.

This "fact of life" — the sociological maturing of children — must be considered and applied both to soccer play and skills development.

Offside

Most of the world's young soccer players do not find themselves in organized, competitive 11-a-side soccer until 10 to 12 years of age. Therefore, it is during "the Golden Age" that coaches have to think seriously about how the offside rule is to be introduced to the young player.

Without question, the offside law is the most complicated one in soccer. Some people, in frustration, have suggested the law should be removed. However, this is not possible. Without the offside law, the 11-a-side game — the way players are deployed and the spaces utilized — would be unrecognizable from the game we play today.

It is a necessary and exciting (and controversial) part of 11-a-side soccer, and the rule and its tactical implications need to be introduced by the coach skillfully and knowledgeably.

The emphasis of this book has been on "skills development" during "the Golden Age" and on "combined play" in small groups to develop an understanding of the principles of offense and defense.

We deliberated as to whether to include the teaching and coaching of "Offside" and decided against it. It would require a lengthy segment to deal properly and fully with this important and influential rule.

Instead, there is separate booklet "Teaching Offside," which concentrates specifically on the offside rule — its interpretation, how and when it should be introduced to young soccer players, the tactical advantages that can be obtained by a team with a thorough knowledge of the law, and practices to teach the offside rule and how to gain the "offside" advantages.

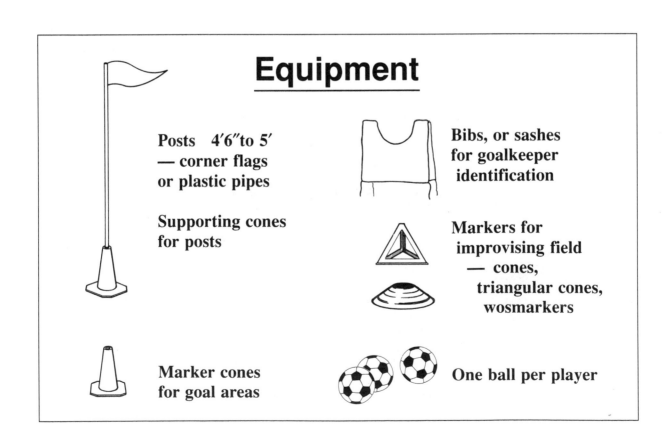

Equipment

Posts   4'6"to 5'
— corner flags
or plastic pipes

Supporting cones
for posts

Marker cones
for goal areas

Bibs, or sashes
for goalkeeper
identification

Markers for
improvising field
— cones,
triangular cones,
wosmarkers

One ball per player

Not The Golden Age of Heading!

Heading a ball is one of the few alien skills of soccer. Nobody in their right mind would choose to be struck on the head. Yet it can be one of the most spectacular and exciting plays in the game. Any adult field player who has poor heading skills is a weak link in the team.

However, recent medical research has cast doubts on the desirability of repetitive heading practice

for players under 12 years of age — particularly with high balls or services from a distance. It appears there could be the risk of permanent damage to the spine arising from the compaction effect of heading the ball.

This is not a medical manual. There is no qualified, expert opinion in this area. But there is enough experience in soccer here to know that the heading skills can be left for intensive development until the next age phase (Early Teens) — particularly as the skill of heading under challenge is something older player can cope with better than a non-discerning youngster. So why take the risks?

Our recommendation is for coaches of 9, 10, and 11 year olds to carefully introduce the correct technique of heading the ball from a gentle service using only a quality hand-stitched leather or synthetic leather ball. It's strongly recommended you do not use a laminated (plastic) ball.

Heading can be included as part of the warm-up or can be used in various relay forms, but with a simple service as shown in the examples.

Bibliography

Coaching to Win – Soccer for the Young Player
Coaching 6, 7, and 8 Year Olds
Teaching Offside
The FIFA World Football Youth Academy Manual

Sources for Teaching and Coaching Books and Videos:

World of Soccer Ltd., Vancouver, B.C.
Soccer Learning Systems, San Ramon, California
Soccer Books, California Youth Soccer Association (North)
Washington State Youth Soccer Association

PLANNING A SEASON'S PROGRAM

Coaches have been encouraged to plan each practice session: to know what each one intends to accomplish (objectives), and what practices and methods are to be used.

The same thinking should be applied on a long-term basis by planning a Season's Program. One week should progress into the next with continuity both in the coaching and the practices — **but** with the clear recognition that everything is subject to review and to reorganization.

Perhaps by using the "Soccer Sandwich" as the basis for each session, the coach can devise a simple formula for the Season's Plan such as the one below. This kind of advance planning will pay dividends.

Overall Objectives for Season: _____

_____

_____

Theme for first 4 weeks: _____

Methods and practices to be used:

Week 1	Week 2	Week 3	Week 4
_____	_____	_____	_____
_____	_____	_____	_____
_____	_____	_____	_____

Review of four weeks: _____

_____

(Do not complete Weeks 5 – 8 until review of Weeks 1 – 4)

Week 5	Week 6	Week 7	Week 8
_____	_____	_____	_____
_____	_____	_____	_____
_____	_____	_____	_____

Review of four weeks: _____

_____